– THE COLLECTOR'S SERIES –
Volume 42

- a taste of regional -
ITALIAN CUISINE

– BY SUSAN SLACK –

The
AMERICAN
★ COOKING ★
GUILD™

DEDICATION
In memory of our mother, Betty Fuller, who loved Italy.

ACKNOWLEDGMENTS

Design	Kristin Moore
Illustrations	Dee Bradney
Map of Italy	Kristin Moore
Cover photo	Burwell & Burwell

ISBN 0-942320-54-9

FOR A CATALOG OF
COOKBOOKS WRITE TO:

The American Cooking Guild
3600-K South Congress Avenue
Boynton Beach, FL 33426-8488

a taste of regional
ITALIAN CUISINE

ANTIPASTO
before the meal
- 7 -

PRIMI PIATTI
pasta, soup, rice
and polenta
- 19 -

SECONDO PIATTI
meats, poultry
and fish
- 33 -

VERDUE E INSALATA
vegetables and
salads
- 41 -

PIZZA E PAN
pizza and
hearth breads
- 49 -

I DOLCI
sweets and fruits
- 55 -

Italian Cuisine

Italian cooking has never been more popular in America! The abundance and variety of Italy's fabled gastronomy has captivated our tastes and imaginations. We have developed a passion for tortellini, risotto, focaccia and espresso. Our insatiable appetite for great Italian food is further tempted by the relaxed Italian approach to dining. Menus are given a great deal of thought. The food is carefully prepared and eaten in leisurely fashion. Eat a little, talk a little! Eat a little, talk a little! A good Italian meal promises to satisfy the appetite for camaraderie as well as tickle the taste buds.

Italian cuisine has evolved since the days of Imperial Rome. Conquering armies returned from long campaigns with exotic new foods and spices. The Greeks brought olives, perfumed honey, spit-roasted lamb and the art of wine making and bread baking to Southern Italy. The Arabs left Sicily great culinary legacies: citrus fruits, sugar, confectionery, ice cream, saffron and couscous. The French influence on Italian cuisine was significant; from it sprang the great monzús who were treasured Sicilian master chefs trained in France.

This is the foundation upon which modern Italian cooking is built. Because of its politics and terrain,

Italy was divided into independent city states; only since 1861 has there been unification. Italian cuisine is a rich tapestry of diverse cooking styles from Italy's 20 regions. Unique culinary customs, local dialects and strong regional pride are golden threads woven tightly into the fabric. Some dishes are still associated with a single city; many foods are tied so closely to the land they can't be authentically produced anywhere else.

Italian cooking sprang from peasant's kitchens but acquired new sophistication from the royal courts of the Medicis in Florence, the Renaissance Popes and other great Italian families. In Italy, the dawn of the Renaissance initiated a period of culinary pre-eminence that inspired France to begin the development of modern French cuisine. Coffee and sugar were introduced to Europe through Italian ports; pasta and cheesecake were also Italian gifts.

Because Italian cuisine is so varied, there isn't room here to present every regional specialty. But you can enjoy a tantalizing taste of cucina casalinga, everyday home cooking, which is some of the finest cuisine Italy has to offer. The recipes are adaptable, easy and delicious; perfect for entertaining. Buon appetito!

Let's cook!

A Culinary Journey

Italy is a small country running 700 miles from north to south, yet it is a land of varied geography, culture and cuisines. Because there are 20 regions with differences in ingredients and cooking techniques, a single cuisine is hard to identify. Common dishes can vary dramatically from north to south. In northern Italy, cattle feed on rich grazing lands; butter and cream are used heavily in cooking. The cuisine is influenced by French, Swiss and Austrian neighbors. Specialties include rice from the fertile Po Valley, white truffles, polenta, rich cheese, game and porcini mushrooms. From Emilia Romagna, gastronomic capital of the agricultural north, comes fresh egg pasta, Parmesan, prosciutto and balsamic vinegar.

The cuisines of central Italy are less complicated. Thick soups, fine beef, pork, pecorino, artichokes, salads, fish soups and chili-laced cheeses are at their finest. Bread often replaces the pasta course.

The sun-parched south has a rugged terrain unsuitable for cattle farming. The rich volcanic soil brings forth some of Italy's best produce. Olive oil, pizza, pork, dried pasta, pulses, sardines, tuna, anchovies and a touch of chilies are staple foods. Sicily, the largest Mediterranean island, has a sophisticated, exotic cuisine influenced by ancient Greek, North African, French and Spanish civilizations. Pecorino, game, hearty breads and fresh wild herbs dominate the cuisine of windswept Sardinia, the area's second largest island.

ANTIPASTO

- before the meal -

ANTIPASTO PARTY

BRUSCHETTA

CROSTINI

SICILIAN OLIVE
RELISH

ROASTED BELL
PEPPERS

CROSTINI WITH
CHEESE TORTA
AND MARINATED
BELL PEPPERS

ARTICHOKE
RELISH WITH
SUN-DRIED
TOMATOES
AND OLIVES

MARINATED
SLICED BEEF
WITH ARUGULA

MARINATED
SHRIMP
WITH LEMON
AND OLIVES

MARINATED
MOZZARELLA
WITH HERBS

SAUTÉED WILD
MUSHROOMS

GRILLED GARLIC
BREAD WITH
FRESH TOMATO
RELISH

Antipasto Party

Antipasti may have evolved from the Roman practice of serving small dishes of condiments before a meal. Pasto means "meal"; antipasto means "before the meal."

Antipasti make wonderful party hors d'oeuvres. Once the food is presented, the service is minimal. The recipes can be prepared in advance. Balance is integral to a good menu. These recipes offer pleasing taste contrasts—spicy and mild, hot and cold, textural and smooth. Some antipasti are light and refreshing; others more substantial.

The antipasto we are most familiar with is a platter of sliced cured meats or <u>affettato misto</u>. It is usually the centerpiece of a lunchtime buffet. You might include prosciutto, salami and copa, a rustic version of prosciutto. Mortadella (with pistachios) is a prototype for American bologna. Plan on 3 or 4 types of thinly sliced meats. Arrange them decoratively on a large platter. Around the periphery arrange piles of Sicilian, Niçoise or Kalamata olives and homemade or ready-made pickled vegetables such as peperoncini (chilies), mushrooms, artichoke hearts, tiny onions, carrot sticks or green beans. The composition of your platter will resemble a colorful Venetian tile mosaic!

MENU:

Cured Meat Platter with Pickled Vegetables

Crostini with Cheese Torta and Marinated Bell Peppers

Artichoke Relish with Sun-Dried Tomatoes and Olives

Marinated Shrimp with Lemon and Olives

Potato Focaccia

Italian Bread Sticks

Fresh Fruit, Wines, Acqua Minerale

Bruschetta

Bruschetta, or Italian-style garlic bread, is as popular today as it was 2,000 years ago when the Romans grilled thick slices of rustic bread over wood fires. Grilled, saltless Tuscan bread is called <u>fettunta</u> or "oiled slice." Cut bread slices 3/4- to 1-inch thick from a crusty, chewy Italian or French peasant-style loaf. Over an outdoor barbecue or under the broiler, grill bread lightly on both sides. Rub one side of each piece with crushed fresh garlic; brush with extra virgin olive oil. For extra flavor, add fresh herbs to the oil. Serve plain or as an antipasto or first course topped with sliced cured meats, melted cheese, white beans, sautéed or grilled vegetables or salad.

Crostini

Crostini means "a little crust." More delicate than bruschetta, the bread is sliced or cut in shapes, toasted and embellished with savory toppings. Cut 1/2-inch slices from a crusty baguette or chewy peasant-style bread. Cut large slices in half. Toast on a baking sheet in a preheated 300° oven for 20 to 25 minutes. When golden brown rub with garlic, if desired; brush with extra virgin olive oil or melted butter. Bread can be pan-fried in oil or butter. Diminutive slices of crostini are good topped with roasted peppers, cheese, fresh tomato slices, fresh herbs, sautéed mushrooms or chicken liver paté. Plain crostini can be served as croutons with salad or soup.

HINTS: For a leaner version of bruschetta or crostini, omit the olive oil or butter and lightly spray the crispy slices with olive mist cooking spray.

Roasted garlic has a creamy texture and a mellow, nutty taste, different from raw or sautéed garlic. Break apart 2 garlic bulbs; place cloves in a pan. Coat with olive oil or cooking spray. Cover; bake in a 400° oven for 25 minutes, until soft and golden. Cool; press cloves to squeeze out soft garlic.

Sicilian Olive Relish

This delicious nibble can be coarsely chopped and stirred into bean salads or sandwiches such as the muffuletta, an Italian version of a New Orleans sub.

2 CUPS CAULIFLOWER FLORETS

1/2 POUND LARGE STUFFED GREEN OLIVES, LIGHTLY MASHED (ABOUT 2 CUPS)

2 THIN CARROTS, DIAGONALLY CUT IN 1/4-INCH SLICES

1 RED BELL PEPPER, CUBED

4 PICKLED PEPPERS (PEPERONCINI) OR PICKLE SALAD

2 STALKS CELERY, DIAGONALLY CUT IN 1/4-INCH SLICES

3 TABLESPOONS CAPERS

1/3 CUP OLIVE OIL

3 TABLESPOONS RED WINE VINEGAR

1 TEASPOON DRIED OREGANO

2 TABLESPOONS CHOPPED FRESH PARSLEY

2 LARGE GARLIC CLOVES, MINCED

Blanch cauliflower in boiling water 1 minute; cool in iced water and drain well; pat dry. Combine with all the remaining ingredients. Store in an airtight container in the refrigerator up to 2 weeks, stirring occasionally.

GOOD FOOD, GOOD HEALTH

The low-fat Mediterranean diet is one we can all live with—for a long time! Healthful, delicious meals are built around a diet high in complex carbohydrates—pasta, grains, dried beans, fresh vegetables and fruits. Olive oil, used since ancient times, is the preferred cooking fat and condiment. Studies indicate olive oil, a monounsaturated fat, helps protect the heart from disease. Highly digestible, it has the same number of calories as other oils, but a small amount goes further because it has flavor.

SERVES 4 AS AN ANTIPASTO OR SIDE DISH

Roasted Bell Peppers

Peppers came to Italy from the New World. The special flavor of roasted peppers, especially ripe, sweet red ones, will enhance your sauces, salads or pasta dishes. Enjoy them on slices of grilled garlic bread. Peppers roasted over a hardwood charcoal fire lend a smoky nuance to your favorite dishes.

| 4 OR 5 LARGE BELL PEPPERS | (RED, YELLOW, GREEN OR A COMBINATION) |

Place peppers on a foil-lined broiler pan; place under a hot broiler. Watch carefully, turning continually as the surfaces begin to char and blister. Remove pan from oven. Wrap foil securely around the peppers or seal inside a heavy brown paper bag. Steam from the hot peppers helps release the skin from the pulp.

When cool, remove skins, stems and seeds. Place in a jar and top with olive oil. Refrigerate; eat within 10 days. Freeze for longer storage.

MAKES 4 TO 5 ROASTED PEPPERS

Crostini with Cheese Torta and Marinated Bell Peppers

A combination of dazzling colors, the bell
pepper topping turns this cheese torta
into a spectacular party appetizer!

2 LARGE ROASTED BELL PEPPERS
(RED AND YELLOW), PAGE 11

2 TABLESPOONS BALSAMIC
OR RED WINE VINEGAR

2 TABLESPOONS EXTRA
VIRGIN OLIVE OIL

1 TABLESPOON EACH MINCED
FRESH PARSLEY AND BASIL

1 TABLESPOON CAPERS

1 SMALL CLOVE GARLIC,
FINELY MINCED

SALT AND FRESHLY GROUND
BLACK PEPPER, TO TASTE

1 (8-OUNCE) PACKAGE CREAM
CHEESE, ROOM TEMPERATURE

1 (4-OUNCE) PACKAGE FETA
CHEESE FLAVORED WITH BASIL
AND TOMATO, OR PLAIN FETA

3 OUNCES FRESH
YOUNG GOAT CHEESE

2 TABLESPOONS TOASTED
PINE NUTS

FRESH BASIL, FOR GARNISH

PLAIN CROSTINI, PAGE 9

Dice roasted bell peppers into squares. Combine with
vinegar, oil, herbs, capers and garlic. Add salt and
pepper. Marinate 30 minutes. In a small bowl, blend
cream cheese, feta and goat cheese until smooth.
Shape into a mound on a large serving plate; slightly
flatten the top. Pour peppers over cheese; garnish
with pine nuts and basil. Surround with crostini.

MAKES 6 SERVINGS

Artichoke Relish with Sun-Dried Tomatoes and Olives

This sunny Mediterranean relish can be
mixed into bean salads, spooned over
grilled swordfish, tuna, lamb chops or
veal or spread on focaccia.

1 (9-OUNCE) PACKAGE FROZEN
ARTICHOKE HEARTS, COOKED,
CUT IN HALF LENGTHWISE

1/3 CUP OIL-PACKED, SUN-DRIED
TOMATOES, CUT IN STRIPS

1/4 CUP NIÇOISE OLIVES OR
1/3 CUP KALAMATA OLIVES,
PITTED, CUT IN LARGE PIECES

1/2 CUP DICED, ROASTED
YELLOW OR RED BELL PEPPER

1 TABLESPOON CAPERS

2 TABLESPOONS MINCED
FRESH HERBS (BASIL,
OREGANO, OR PARSLEY)

2 TABLESPOONS
BALSAMIC VINEGAR

1/4 CUP EXTRA
VIRGIN OLIVE OIL

SALT AND FRESHLY GROUND
BLACK PEPPER, TO TASTE

Combine all ingredients in a medium
bowl. Serve at once or cover and
refrigerate. The relish tastes best
at room temperature.

ITALIAN MEALS
Breakfast is of little importance; a quick start might be biscotti
or butter and bread with caffé e latte (coffee and milk). Pranzo
famigliare (family lunch) is the most substantial meal of the day,
usually two courses, fruit and cheese. The evening meal or cena is
lighter, perhaps soup and one course. Upper classes may serve pranzo in the evening and cena as a late-night supper. An abbreviated
one-course meal, piatto unico, is a newer concept. Once deemed
peasant food, pasta and pizza are now fashionable "fast food."

MAKES ABOUT 2 CUPS.

Marinated Sliced Beef with Arugula

Thin slices of zesty marinated beef tenderloin are especially delicious on crostini made with sun-dried tomatoes or black olive bread. Peppery arugula (rucola) has a taste assertive enough to match the marinade.

1 POUND BEEF TENDERLOIN, TRIMMED

1/3 CUP EXTRA VIRGIN OLIVE OIL

JUICE OF 1 LEMON

1 TABLESPOON EACH FRESH MINCED PARSLEY, BASIL AND OREGANO OR MARJORAM

1 TABLESPOON CAPERS

1 CLOVE GARLIC, FINELY MINCED

SALT AND FRESHLY GROUND BLACK PEPPER

CROSTINI, PAGE 9

ONE BUNCH FRESH ARUGULA OR WATERCRESS

Heat a medium heavy skillet over high heat. Coat the meat with olive oil. Sear on all sides until crusty and brown. Cook until the meat is rare or registers 120°. Remove pan from heat; the temperature of the meat will rise slightly as it stands. Cool completely. Wrap tightly and chill 2 hours or overnight. Cut meat into thin slices and arrange in a shallow serving dish. In a small bowl, whisk the remaining olive oil, lemon juice, herbs, capers and garlic. Drizzle mixture over meat; season lightly with salt and pepper. Cover and marinate 30 minutes; refrigerate for a longer period. To serve, gently mix meat with dressing. Top each toast with a piece of arugula and 1 or 2 slices of meat. Season with salt and pepper, if desired.

MAKES 6 TO 8 SERVINGS

Marinated Shrimp with Lemon and Olives

Try this dish using poached squid
rings or sliced sea scallops.

1 1/2 POUNDS MEDIUM SHRIMP

2 TABLESPOONS FRESH LEMON JUICE

1/3 CUP EXTRA VIRGIN OLIVE OIL

1 LARGE GARLIC CLOVE, CRUSHED

SALT AND FRESHLY GROUND BLACK PEPPER, TO TASTE

1 TABLESPOON FRESH MINCED PARSLEY

1 TABLESPOON FRESH MINCED CHIVES

1/4 TEASPOON CRUSHED RED CHILIES

1/2 CUP NIÇOISE OR KALAMATA OLIVES

1 LEMON, CUT IN SLICES

Bring a large pot of water to boil over high heat.
Cook shrimp for 2 minutes. Drain well; peel and
devein. Place shrimp in a large bowl with the
remaining ingredients. Cover bowl and chill 1
hour or overnight. Place in a serving dish;
garnish with decorative lemon slices.

THE SOUTHERN ITALIAN-AMERICAN CONNECTION

In the late 1800s, Italian cuisine came to the United States
with the great influx of Italian immigrants, many from the
southern regions. Village-oriented communities sprang up, com-
posed of neighborhood groups from the "old country." Each com-
munity fostered the culinary heritage and rich traditions of its
ancestral home. Yet subtle changes in the cooking began to take
place as indigenous ingredients, new cooking methods and traditions were incorporated. Over the years, the regional cuisines
became unified, creating a new Italian-American cuisine.

MAKES 6 SERVINGS

Marinated Mozzarella with Herbs

Marinated mozzarella on grilled bread is a filling quick snack or lunch. Dress up each serving with a confetti topping of diced marinated red, yellow and green bell peppers. Perishable buffalo's milk mozzarella is not found often outside of southern Italy. You can substitute fresh cow's milk mozzarella.

1 POUND FRESH MOZZARELLA, DRAINED, THINLY SLICED

2 TABLESPOONS FRESH SHREDDED BASIL LEAVES

2 TABLESPOONS CHOPPED ITALIAN PARSLEY

1/4 CUP EXTRA VIRGIN OLIVE OIL

SALT AND FRESHLY GROUND BLACK PEPPER, TO TASTE

1/2 TEASPOON RED PEPPER FLAKES, IF DESIRED

CROSTINI, PAGE 9

Overlap cheese slices in a large shallow dish. Top with remaining ingredients. Coat cheese slices with the marinade. Cover tightly and refrigerate at least 2 hours. Turn onto a serving platter; serve with grilled bread.

ITALIAN MEALS

The formal meal is presented in "service a la russe." Small diverse courses of equal importance are presented separately. A light starter or antipasto might be fresh melon wrapped with prosciutto. Restaurant antipasti are far more elaborate.

MAKES 6 SERVINGS

Sautéed Wild Mushrooms

Wild mushrooms are a specialty of northern Italy; golden brown porcini is the undisputed favorite. Rehydrate dried mushrooms with a 30-minute soak in hot water. Rinse well; trim off the tough parts. Strain soaking liquid through a coffee filter; save for pasta sauces or soups. At a fancy restaurant, an appetizer of sautéed wild mushrooms on bruschetta costs a king's ransom! Try it at home; embellish the top with shaved Parmesan cheese.

1 TABLESPOON OLIVE OIL

1 POUND MIXED WILD MUSHROOMS (PORCINI, SHIITAKE, MORELS, OYSTER, CHANTERELLES) OR A WILD AND DOMESTIC BLEND

1 GARLIC CLOVE, FINELY MINCED

1 TABLESPOON EACH MINCED FRESH MARJORAM AND FRESH CHIVES

1 TO 2 TABLESPOONS BALSAMIC VINEGAR, TO TASTE

SALT AND FRESHLY GROUND BLACK PEPPER, TO TASTE

BRUSCHETTA, PAGE 9

Heat oil in a large heavy skillet over high heat. Sauté mushrooms 4 minutes or until liquid from the mushrooms has evaporated. Stir in garlic, herbs and vinegar; cook 30 seconds more. Remove to a heated serving dish. Add salt and pepper. Serve on grilled bread.

MAKES 4 TO 5 SERVINGS

Grilled Garlic Bread with Fresh Tomato Relish

Make this dish with plump juicy tomatoes picked right off the vine. You know the kind; with every bite, the juice drips exquisitely down your chin.

1 POUND FRESH TOMATOES, PEELED, SEEDED, DICED

1 TABLESPOON BALSAMIC VINEGAR

1 TABLESPOON EXTRA VIRGIN OLIVE OIL

1 TABLESPOON MINCED FRESH BASIL OR OREGANO LEAVES

1 SMALL GARLIC CLOVE, MINCED

SALT AND FRESHLY GROUND BLACK PEPPER, TO TASTE

BRUSCHETTA OR CROSTINI, PAGE 9

Combine all the ingredients, except the grilled bread, in a medium bowl. Marinate 30 minutes at room temperature. Prepare bruschetta; spoon relish on top. Also delicious spooned over grilled eggplant.

COOKING TIPS:

These techniques are flavor-builders for fine Italian dishes.

BATTUTO: This is the first step of many dishes. Finely chopped garlic and onion are lightly sautéed in olive oil, butter, pancetta (bacon) or lard. When lightly colored and aromatic, these ingredients are called a soffritto. Optional ingredients: parsley, pepper, celery, and carrots.

INSAPORIRE: This technique adds real flavor to vegetable dishes. Insaporire means "to make more tasty." Vegetables are added to sautéed onions and garlic and cooked to "make tasty." The vegetable is used for soup, sauce or pasta. This step creates a flavor-depth that otherwise might be missing.

MAKES 6 SERVINGS

PRIMI PIATTI

- pasta, soup, rice and polenta -

MUSHROOM RAVIOLI WITH RED PEPPER SAUCE AND WALNUTS	POLENTA
PESTO	SEAFOOD SPAGHETTI IN A BAG
LINGUINI WITH PESTO AND GREEN BEANS	RAGU ALLA BOLOGNESE
FETTUCCINE AL POMODORO	RISOTTO ALLA NAPOLETANA
EGGPLANT AND SAUSAGE PENNE	FARFALLE IN SUN-DRIED TOMATO SAUCE
MINESTRONE	LASAGNA PINWHEELS STUFFED WITH SPINACH
CHICKEN SOUP WITH ESCAROLE	

Mushroom Ravioli with Red Pepper Sauce and Walnuts

I like to serve pasta in colorful Vietri plates and bowls with bunnies and birds frolicking around the edges. The silky red pepper sauce makes a sensational dip for raw vegetables or tortellini made with tomatoes or spinach pasta. For a spectacular presentation, skewer red and green tortellini and arrange them around the sauce for dipping.

1 CUP CHOPPED ROASTED RED BELL PEPPERS, ROOM TEMPERATURE, PAGE 11

1 GARLIC CLOVE, MINCED, OR ROASTED GARLIC, TO TASTE

4 OUNCES MASCARPONE OR CREAM CHEESE, ROOM TEMPERATURE

SALT AND GROUND WHITE PEPPER, TO TASTE

8 TO 10 OUNCES FRESH OR FROZEN MUSHROOM OR CHEESE RAVIOLI, TORTELLINI OR AGNOLOTTI, PARTIALLY THAWED IF FROZEN

2 TABLESPOONS WALNUT OIL (LORIVA) OR BASIL-FLAVORED OLIVE OIL

2 TABLESPOONS FINELY CHOPPED TOASTED WALNUTS

8 FRESH BASIL LEAVES

In the work bowl of a food processor fitted with the steel blade, process peppers and garlic until smooth.

Add mascarpone; process to blend. Add salt and pepper. Cook ravioli in a large pot of salted water 4 to 6 minutes or until tender. Drain; coat with oil.

Arrange several ravioli on each plate and spoon sauce on top. Garnish with walnuts and basil leaves.

MAKES 4 FIRST-COURSE OR
2 MAIN-COURSE SERVINGS

Pesto

Of Persian origin, this aromatic basil sauce is a specialty of Liguria on the Mediterranean. Parsley helps preserve the sauce's green color; a few drops of lemon juice helps too. Use pesto on your favorite pasta, pizza or gnocchi or in minestrone, potato salad or mayonnaise.

2 LARGE GARLIC CLOVES, PEELED	2 TABLESPOONS FRESHLY GRATED PARMESAN CHEESE
1 PACKED CUP FRESH BASIL LEAVES	2 TABLESPOONS FRESHLY GRATED PECORINO CHEESE OR PARMESAN
1/4 CUP FRESH PARSLEY SPRIGS	1/4 CUP VIRGIN OLIVE OIL, AS NEEDED
3 TABLESPOONS PINE NUTS OR WALNUTS, LIGHTLY TOASTED	1/2 TEASPOON SALT, TO TASTE

Place garlic, basil, parsley, pine nuts and cheeses in the work bowl of a food processor fitted with the steel blade. Process to chop ingredients. Slowly add oil to create a paste. Add salt and use immediately. Can be refrigerated 2 weeks in a jar with olive oil drizzled on top of the pesto. Freeze for longer keeping.

PERFECT PASTA

Cook pasta in ample water to prevent gumminess. Use 3 to 4 quarts of water with 2 teaspoons salt for up to 1/2 pound of pasta. Use 4 quarts of water with 1 tablespoon salt for 1/2 to 1 pound of pasta. Do not add oil; pasta will be slick. When the water comes to a rolling boil, add pasta. Cook uncovered, stirring once or twice. After 4 or 5 minutes, begin tasting pasta in 1 to 2 minute intervals. Pasta should be cooked al dente or "to the tooth." This means it is still chewy but the hard white center has disappeared. Drain in a colander; do not rinse. Place pasta into the warm pot for immediate saucing. Fresh pasta cooks in less time.

MAKES 1 CUP SAUCE

Linguini with Pesto and Green Beans

Pasta and pesto are a natural pair and even more delicious tossed with fresh green beans and tangy sun-dried tomatoes. For a change, omit the green beans and substitute thinly sliced sautéed zucchini.

$^1/_2$ POUND FRESH THIN GREEN BEANS, ENDS TRIMMED, SLICED IN HALF DIAGONALLY

8 OUNCES DRIED LINGUINE OR SPAGHETTI, COOKED AL DENTE

$^1/_2$ CUP PESTO, PAGE 21, OR TO TASTE

$^1/_2$ CUP OIL-PACKED SUN-DRIED TOMATOES OR 1 ROASTED RED BELL PEPPER, PAGE 11, CUT IN THIN STRIPS

SALT AND FRESHLY GROUND BLACK PEPPER

FRESHLY GRATED PARMESAN, PECORINO OR ASIAGO CHEESE

Bring a pot of water to boil; cook green beans 8 to 10 minutes or until crisp-tender. Drain well, then pat dry. Toss cooked pasta with pesto, green beans and sun-dried tomatoes. Add salt and pepper. Divide among heated serving bowls. Serve at once with the cheese.

HINT: Italians often eat their pasta lightly coated with sauce; a portion of sauce is saved for the top. Hot pasta can be tossed first with butter and grated cheese in the cooking pot before the sauce is added. This is a flavor bonus, especially when the sauce is a simple one with few ingredients.

MAKES 4 FIRST-COURSE SERVINGS
OR 2 MAIN-COURSE SERVINGS

Fettuccine al Pomodoro

Often called "marinara" sauce, this versatile tomato sauce can be mixed with your favorite pasta or used as a topping for fried foods and pizza. Gerrie Cascione warms homegrown cooked Italian green beans in her sauce and then serves it with spaghetti and Parmesan. She cuts the beans into 2-inch pieces; regular string beans will work as well.

1/4 CUP OLIVE OIL

1 SMALL RED ONION, FINELY CHOPPED

3 GARLIC CLOVES, MINCED

3 TO 3-1/2 POUNDS RIPE TOMATOES, PEELED, SEEDED, CHOPPED, OR 2 (28-OUNCE) CANS TOMATOES, DRAINED, CHOPPED

1/2 TEASPOON SUGAR

3 TABLESPOONS MINCED FRESH HERBS (PARSLEY, BASIL, ROSEMARY, MARJORAM)

SALT AND FRESHLY GROUND BLACK PEPPER, TO TASTE

3/4 POUND FRESH FETTUCCINE OR 1/2 POUND DRIED NOODLES

2 TABLESPOONS BUTTER

1 CUP FRESHLY GRATED PARMESAN CHEESE, PECORINO OR ASIAGO

Heat oil in a heavy saucepan over medium heat. Sauté onion and garlic 5 minutes, stirring often until translucent. Add tomatoes and sugar. Reduce heat to low. Simmer 20 minutes, stirring often. Blend in herbs, salt and pepper. Keep warm. Cook fresh noodles in boiling salted water 2 minutes; dried noodles take longer. Drain and mix in butter and 1/2 the sauce. Divide among heated serving bowls; top with remaining sauce and cheese.

TIP: If your tomato sauce lacks intensity, squeeze in 1 to 2 tablespoons concentrated tomato paste or sun-dried tomato paste from a tube. It is available in the imported food section of fine markets.

MAKES 3 CUPS OF SAUCE, 6 FIRST-COURSE SERVINGS, 3 MAIN-COURSE SERVINGS

Eggplant and Sausage Penne

In Italy, hollow pasta is collectively called mac-cheroni or macaroni. This chunky eggplant sauce is delicious over macaroni such as penne or mostaccioli (slant cut macaroni), cavatappi (spiral macaroni) or ziti (slightly curved or straight tubes).

2 TABLESPOONS OLIVE OIL

1 MEDIUM-SMALL ONION, CHOPPED

2 LARGE GARLIC CLOVES, MINCED

1 MEDIUM RED OR GREEN BELL PEPPER, CHOPPED

3/4 POUND BULK ITALIAN SAUSAGE OR LINKS, WITH CASINGS REMOVED

1 SMALL EGGPLANT (3/4 POUND), CUT IN 1/2-INCH CUBES

2 POUNDS RIPE TOMATOES, PEELED, SEEDED, CHOPPED, OR 1 (28-OUNCE) CAN CHOPPED TOMATOES IN JUICE

1/4 CUP FRESH MINCED HERBS (PARSLEY, OREGANO, BASIL)

12 KALAMATA OLIVES, PITTED, QUARTERED

SALT AND FRESHLY GROUND BLACK PEPPER, TO TASTE

1 POUND DRIED PENNE OR ZITI

1 CUP FRESHLY GRATED RICOTTA SALATA, PECORINO OR PARMESAN CHEESE

In a medium saucepan heat oil. Sauté onion, garlic and bell pepper 5 minutes, stirring often. Add sausage; stir to break up. Add eggplant, tomatoes, herbs and olives. Cover pot and reduce heat to low. Simmer 45 minutes. Add salt and pepper. Keep warm. Cook pasta in boiling salted water, referring to package directions. Drain. Serve in heated bowls with sauce and grated cheese to taste.

TIP: For each tablespoon of fresh chopped herbs, you can substitute 1 teaspoon dried herb leaves. Whole leaves offer more flavor than finely ground herbs. Check your dried herb supply regularly to make sure it is fresh.

MAKES 4 TO 5 SERVINGS

Minestrone

Minestrone is a soup specialty of central and northern Italy. The soup might be ladled over slices of grilled country-style bread. The roots of this practice may stem from medieval times when castle servants made soup from wild herbs and recycled trenchers, which were large pieces of bread used as serving plates. To make <u>minestrone alla genovese</u>, stir in 2 tablespoons Pesto (page 21) before serving.

1/4 CUP OLIVE OIL

1 MEDIUM ONION, CHOPPED

2 CLOVES GARLIC, MINCED

1/4 SMALL HEAD SAVOY CABBAGE, SHREDDED (2 TO 3 CUPS)

2 STALKS CELERY, CHOPPED

2 CARROTS, CHOPPED

1 QUART RICH BEEF BROTH

1 QUART WATER

4 OUNCES TOMATO PASTE

1/4 CUP MINCED FRESH HERBS (PARSLEY, BASIL OR MARJORAM)

3 SMALL ZUCCHINI, CUT INTO HALF-MOON SLICES

1 CUP SLICED FRESH OR FROZEN ITALIAN GREEN BEANS OR REGULAR GREEN BEANS

2 CUPS OR 1 (19-OUNCE) CAN COOKED CANNELLINI BEANS OR 1 CAN GREAT NORTHERN BEANS

2 CUP COOKED CRANBERRY BEANS OR 1 (16-OUNCE) CAN PINTO BEANS

6 OUNCES GENOA SALAMI, DICED IN SMALL CUBES

1/2 CUP SMALL PASTA SHAPES: CONCHIGLIETTE (SMALL SHELLS), CAVATELLI (ELONGATED SHELLS OR DRY GNOCCHI) OR ORECCHIETTE ("LITTLE EARS")

SALT AND FRESHLY GROUND BLACK PEPPER, TO TASTE

FRESHLY GRATED PARMESAN CHEESE

In a large saucepan, heat oil. Sauté onion and garlic 2 to 3 minutes. Add cabbage, celery and carrots. Sauté 5 minutes. Add broth, water, tomato paste and herbs. Partially cover pan and simmer 30 minutes. Add zucchini, beans and salami; cook 15 minutes. Add macaroni; cook until al dente. Add salt and pepper. Serve in large bowls with grated cheese.

MAKES 6 TO 8 SERVINGS

Chicken Soup with Escarole

Simple and filling! Good broth is the foundation for a delicious soup. Homemade is best, providing a rich flavor base. In a pinch, enrich canned broth by simmering it with chicken parts, vegetables and seasonings.

5 CUPS OF STRONG CHICKEN BROTH, PREFERABLY HOMEMADE

1 BUNCH FRESH ESCAROLE, RINSED, TRIMMED, CUT IN HALF

8 OR 9 OUNCES AGNOLOTTI OR TORTELLINI, FRESH OR THAWED IF FROZEN

SALT AND FRESHLY GROUND BLACK PEPPER, TO TASTE

FRESHLY GRATED PARMESAN CHEESE

Simmer chicken broth in a large saucepan over medium-low heat. Cook escarole in boiling salted water 10 minutes. Drain well; cool slightly. Press out liquid, slice and add to broth. Cook stuffed pasta in boiling water 3 or 4 minutes or until al dente. Drain and add to broth. Simmer 1 or 2 minutes more. Add salt and pepper. Serve with grated Parmesan cheese.

ITALIAN MEALS

After antipasto comes <u>primo piatto</u> or the "first plate" of pasta or risotto. Soup might be offered at the evening meal. Often served in a wide, flat bowl, a primo piatto may be called a minestra or "wet course" since it contains sauce or liquid. Antipasti may be served as primi. America has adopted several primi piatti as single-course meals.

MAKES 6 TO 8 SERVINGS

Polenta

Polenta is similar to the rustic American cornmeal mush; prepared Italian-style, it is a culinary delight. In northern Italy, polenta substitutes for pasta or bread. It is also a good side dish for meat. Top with ragu, meat stew or ratatouille for a main dish. For hors d'oeuvres, sauté polenta shapes in butter or bake until crisp; add a savory topping. The double boiler cuts down the need for constant stirring.

3 CUPS BOILING WATER (OR WATER AND CHICKEN BROTH), ADD AS NEEDED	4 TABLESPOONS BUTTER
1 TEASPOON SALT	1/2 CUP GRATED PARMESAN CHEESE, MORE IF DESIRED
1 CUP POLENTA OR COARSE-GRAIN YELLOW CORNMEAL	

Simmer water in a double boiler base. Put the top pan into place; pour in the 3 cups boiling water. Add salt. Whisk in cornmeal slowly to prevent lumps. Cover pan. Cook on low, about 45 minutes to 1 hour, or until polenta is soft and creamy, stirring occasionally. When done, mix in half the butter and Parmesan cheese. Pour into a heated serving bowl. Top with remaining butter and cheese. Serve at once. To make polenta shapes, pour hot polenta into a rectangular baking pan. Chill and cut into desired shapes.

POLENTA TOPPINGS:
Sautéed Wild Mushrooms, page 17
Sautéed greens (broccoli rabe, escarole, chicory)
Sliced, sautéed bell peppers and onions
Chunky tomato sauce, page 52
Ragu alla Bolognese, page 29
4 ounces each gorgonzola and mascarpone,
mashed with 2 Tablespoons chopped walnuts

MAKES 4 SERVINGS

Seafood Spaghetti in a Bag

Seafood and spaghetti are delicious cooked together inside a bag. The cooking method is called cartoccio and is used mainly for baking whole fish with clams, scallops, shrimp and oysters. This version conveniently uses aluminum foil. Scrub mussels well with a stiff brush; remove the mussel beards by pulling them toward the narrow ends.

2 POUNDS LIVE MUSSELS, SCRUBBED, DE-BEARDED, RINSED WELL IN COLD WATER	$^1/_4$ CUP KALAMATA OLIVES, PITS REMOVED
1 CLOVE GARLIC, MINCED	SALT AND FRESHLY GROUND PEPPER, TO TASTE
1 RECIPE CHUNKY TOMATO SAUCE, PAGE 52	$^1/_2$ POUND THIN SPAGHETTI
$^1/_4$ CUP MINCED FRESH PARSLEY	$^1/_2$ POUND RAW SHELLFISH (MEDIUM SHRIMP, PEELED AND DEVEINED, OR SCALLOPS)

Put mussels into a large skillet over medium-high heat. Cover tightly and cook 6 to 8 minutes, shaking pan several times. Discard any mussels that do not open. Remove mussels from shells; keep warm. Strain pan juices through a coffee filter. In a clean saucepan, simmer garlic 3 or 4 minutes. Stir in tomato sauce, parsley, olives, salt and pepper. Bring a large pot of salted water to boil. Preheat oven to 450°. Cook spaghetti until almost al dente. Drain and mix with sauce. Place large double sheets of aluminum foil on a large baking sheet. Spread spaghetti on one half; top with mussels and shellfish. Seal foil tightly. Place sealed packet on baking sheet and bake 10 minutes. Serve immediately. Cut foil open for serving.

MAKES 4 FIRST-COURSE OR
3-MAIN COURSE SERVINGS

Ragu alla Bolognese

The Bologna Chamber of Commerce (in Emilia Romagna) has codified its ragu sauce, rich with ground veal, butter and cream. It is traditionally served with tagliatelle, ribbon-shaped fresh egg noodles similar to fettuccine. In southern ragu, cuts of meat are simmered in tomato sauce. The meats are served on a platter; the sauce mixed with cooked pasta. Southern Italian-Americans often refer to ragu as "gravy."

3 TABLESPOONS OLIVE OIL

1 MEDIUM ONION, FINELY CHOPPED

1 STALK CELERY, FINELY CHOPPED

1 SMALL CARROT, FINELY CHOPPED

2 LARGE GARLIC CLOVES, MINCED

1 POUND LEAN GROUND BEEF, PORK OR VEAL (OR A BLEND)

2 POUNDS RIPE TOMATOES, PEELED, SEEDED, CHOPPED, OR 1 (28-OUNCE) CAN TOMATOES IN JUICE, CHOPPED

1 (7-OUNCE) CAN TOMATO SAUCE

1/4 CUP RED WINE

2 TABLESPOONS FRESH CHOPPED OREGANO OR BASIL

DASH NUTMEG

SALT AND FRESHLY GROUND BLACK PEPPER, TO TASTE

Heat oil in a large saucepan over medium heat. Sauté onion, celery, carrots and garlic. Stir in meat. When browned, add remaining ingredients, except salt and pepper. Reduce heat. Cover pan and simmer 1 hour, stirring occasionally. Add salt and pepper. Serve immediately with pasta, or cool and refrigerate for up to 2 days; freeze for longer storage.

MAKES 4 1/2 CUPS OF SAUCE

Risotto Alla Napoletana

Chef Bruce Sacino has been Executive Chef at the South Carolina Governor's Mansion since 1989. The following recipe is an example of the comforting meals that exemplify the homestyle cuisine of Naples, the city Chef Bruce's grandfather Antonio Sacino immigrated from in the early 1900's.

5 CUPS CHICKEN STOCK, PREFERABLY HOMEMADE

3 TABLESPOONS OLIVE OIL

3/4 CUP SHALLOTS, PEELED AND MINCED

2 TEASPOONS FINELY CHOPPED GARLIC

1 1/2 CUPS PLUM TOMATOES, BLANCHED, PEELED, SEEDED AND CHOPPED

2 CUPS ARBORIO RICE

1 CUP DRY WHITE WINE

2/3 CUP CHOPPED FRESH BASIL LEAVES

1 TABLESPOON FINELY CHOPPED FRESH THYME LEAVES

1 TABLESPOON UNSALTED BUTTER

1/2 POUND FRESHLY-SHAVED PARMESAN

SALT AND PEPPER, TO TASTE

In a medium-size saucepan, bring stock to a boil; lower heat and keep it at a simmer. In a 5 quart saucepan, heat oil over medium-high heat until hot but not smoking. Sauté shallots and garlic until translucent, 4 to 5 minutes. Add tomatoes; sauté 3 minutes.

Stir in rice. Cook about 1 minute, stirring constantly, until well coated with oil. Add wine and cook, stirring constantly, until absorbed. Add 1 cup simmering stock; cook over medium heat, stirring constantly until absorbed. Continue adding stock 1/2 cup at a time, stirring between each addition until the liquid is completely absorbed before adding more. When half the stock is used, add the basil and thyme. Continue until rice is tender and creamy looking, yet still al dente, about 20 minutes. Add butter and cheese. Season with salt and pepper. Serve immediately.

MAKES 6 SERVINGS

Farfalle in Sun-Dried Tomato Sauce

Farfalle resembles butterflies or bow ties, depending on your point of view. Thawed frozen baby green peas can be added to the creamy sauce.

2 TABLESPOONS BUTTER

1 MINCED SHALLOT

2 GARLIC CLOVES, FINELY MINCED

1 CUP HEAVY CREAM

1 CUP PLUM TOMATOES, PEELED, CHOPPED, SEEDED

1 TABLESPOON MINCED FRESH BASIL

1/4 CUP OIL-PACKED SUN-DRIED TOMATOES, CUT IN THIN STRIPS

SALT AND FRESHLY GROUND BLACK PEPPER, TO TASTE

1/2 POUND FARFALLE

FRESHLY GRATED PARMESAN CHEESE

Melt butter in a medium saucepan. Sauté shallot and garlic 30 seconds, stirring constantly. Add cream and tomatoes. Reduce heat; simmer 10 minutes. Stir in basil, sun-dried tomatoes, salt and pepper. Keep warm. Cook the farfalle according package directions. Drain well and mix into the sauce. Divide among heated bowls. Serve with grated Parmesan cheese.

MAKES 4 FIRST-COURSE SERVINGS
OR 2 MAIN-COURSE SERVINGS

Lasagna Pinwheels
Stuffed with Spinach

Some lasagna noodles are thicker than others.
For this recipe, purchase very thin ruffled
noodles. If you are pressed for time, use a jar
of good-quality, store-bought tomato sauce.

3 CUPS MARINARA SAUCE,
FROM THE RECIPE FOR
FETTUCCINE AL POMODORO
PAGE 23, OR OTHER
TOMATO SAUCE

1 BUNCH FRESH SPINACH
(ABOUT 1 1/4 POUNDS),
WELL RINSED

3 TABLESPOONS OLIVE OIL

1 CUP FINELY CHOPPED
RED ONION

1/2 POUND FRESH
MUSHROOMS

2 GARLIC CLOVES, MINCED

PINCH FRESHLY GRATED
NUTMEG

SALT AND FRESHLY GROUND
BLACK PEPPER, TO TASTE

1 CUP RICOTTA CHEESE

5 TABLESPOONS FRESHLY
GRATED PECORINO OR
ASIAGO CHEESE

8 DRIED LASAGNA NOODLES

1 CUP SHREDDED FONTINA
CHEESE OR MOZZARELLA
CHEESE (4 OUNCES)

Prepare sauce. Place spinach in a large pot over high heat.
When wilted, remove from heat and cool. Squeeze out water
and chop. Heat oil in a large skillet. Sauté onions, mushrooms
and garlic until soft. Mix in spinach, nutmeg, salt and pepper.
Cool. Stir in ricotta and 2 tablespoons pecorino. Preheat oven
to 350°. Spread each noodle with 3 tablespoons filling. Roll up
and slice each noodle in half to form circular pieces. Place 2
cups of sauce in a 13-inch by 9-inch pan. Place pinwheels in
sauce, ruffled edges up. Top with 1 cup sauce and remaining
pecorino and fontina. Bake 30 minutes until bubbly.

MAKES 8 FIRST-COURSE SERVINGS OR
4 MAIN-COURSE SERVINGS

SECONDO PIATTI

- meats, poultry and fish -

GRILLED TUSCAN STEAK	GRILLED SALMON WITH PESTO
VEAL CUTLETS WITH HAZELNUTS	CHICKEN BREASTS WITH PROSCIUTTO AND FONTINA
FLORENTINE MEATLOAF	
FLOUNDER MARINARA	GRILLED LAMB CHOPS WITH MINT PESTO

Grilled Tuscan Steak

In Tuscan cuisine, uncomplicated dishes offer maximum flavor! Made from fine Tuscan beef, bistecca alla fiorentina is a very popular dish. Meat-loving Americans appreciate this one too. The only absolute for this dish is to buy top-quality beef. The traditional condiment is a drizzle of extra virgin olive oil. Sautéed wild mushrooms are a fine accompaniment. Serve the steak and mushrooms with a side dish of peppery arugula sautéed in olive oil.

1 PORTERHOUSE STEAK, 1 1/2 INCHES THICK, OR OTHER TENDER CUT

1 TEASPOON BLACK PEPPERCORNS, COARSELY GROUND JUST BEFORE USED

EXTRA VIRGIN OLIVE OIL, PORCINI MUSHROOM OR HERB-FLAVORED OLIVE OIL

SAUTÉED WILD MUSHROOMS, PAGE 17, IF DESIRED

Remove steak from refrigerator 1/2 hour before cooking. Rub ground peppercorns into both sides. Prepare charcoal fire with fragrant hardwoods. Grill steak 4 to 5 minutes on each side for rare, turning only once. While the meat is cooking, sauté mushrooms in a skillet on the grill. Remove meat and drizzle it with olive oil. Wait 5 minutes before carving. Top slices of meat with sautéed mushrooms.

TIP: Do not carve roasted meats or poultry immediately after they are removed from the oven. A 5 to 10-minute "rest" period allows time for the juices to be reabsorbed into the meat.

MAKES 2 SERVINGS

Ueal Cutlets with Hazelnuts

Hazelnut and crumb-coated slices of veal, turkey and tender beef are delicious lightly sautéed. Grate stale Italian or French bread on a hand-held grater or make the crumbs in the food processor. To prevent a soggy fried coating, toast soft fresh crumbs lightly in a heavy skillet until crisp and dry. Try this flavorful crumb mixture as a coating for a rack of lamb.

2 CUPS FRESH BREAD CRUMBS, LIGHTLY TOASTED

1/4 CUP GROUND HAZELNUTS OR BLANCHED ALMONDS

3 TABLESPOONS FINELY MINCED FRESH PARSLEY

1 TABLESPOON FINELY MINCED FRESH SAGE OR MARJORAM

1/4 CUP FRESHLY GRATED PARMESAN CHEESE

1 LARGE GARLIC CLOVE, FINELY MINCED

1/2 TEASPOON SEASONING SALT

SEVERAL DASHES FRESHLY GROUND BLACK PEPPER

1 POUND VEAL CUTLETS OR TURKEY BREAST SLICES, THINLY POUNDED

1 LARGE EGG BEATEN WITH 1 TABLESPOON MILK

2 TABLESPOONS UNSALTED BUTTER

1 TABLESPOON OLIVE OIL, ADD MORE IF NEEDED

1 LEMON, CUT INTO WEDGES

Mix bread crumbs, nuts, herbs, Parmesan, garlic, salt and pepper in a shallow pan. Coat veal with beaten egg, then dredge with seasoned crumbs. Melt butter and oil in a large skillet until hot. Sauté cutlets in batches, about 2 minutes on each side, until crisp and golden brown. Drain on paper towels. Place on a serving platter and garnish with lemon. Serve immediately.

MAKES 4 SERVINGS

Florentine Meatloaf

When 14-year-old Catherine de Medici left Florence
to marry King Henry II of France, her entourage
of chefs encountered spinach for the first time.
From then on, they referred to dishes with spinach
as florentine, which means "bed of spinach" in
French. This moist spinach and beef loaf tastes
even better topped with marinara sauce, from the
recipe for Fettuccine al Pomodoro, page 23.

1 TABLESPOON OLIVE OIL

1 CUP FINELY CHOPPED ONION

1 LARGE GARLIC CLOVE,
FINELY MINCED

1/2 TEASPOON FENNEL SEED

1 (10-OUNCE) PACKAGE
FROZEN CHOPPED SPINACH,
THAWED, SQUEEZED DRY

1 POUND LEAN GROUND BEEF

1/2 POUND HOT OR
SWEET ITALIAN SAUSAGE

1 CUP RICOTTA CHEESE

1/2 CUP FRESH TOMATO
JUICE OR BEEF STOCK

1 LARGE EGG

1/2 CUP FRESH BREAD
CRUMBS

1/4 CUP FRESHLY GRATED
PARMESAN CHEESE

2 TABLESPOONS EACH OF
MINCED FRESH PARSLEY
AND FRESH BASIL

1 TEASPOON SALT

Preheat oven to 350°. Heat oil and sauté onion,
garlic and fennel seed 2 minutes, stirring constantly. Combine with the remaining ingredients.
Shape mixture into a log and place in a shallow
casserole dish. Bake 1 hour or until the ther-
mometer registers 150°. Cool 10 minutes.

MAKES 6 SERVINGS

Flounder Marinara

Serve with a side dish of creamy hot
polenta, page 27.

MARINARA SAUCE, FROM THE RECIPE FOR FETTUCCINE AL POMODORO, PAGE 23	2 TABLESPOONS MINCED FRESH PARSLEY
1/2 CUP SLICED BLACK OLIVES	1 1/2 TO 2 POUNDS FISH FILLETS (FLOUNDER, COD, HADDOCK)
2 TABLESPOONS CAPERS	

Prepare marinara sauce. Pour into a large
skillet over medium-low heat. Stir in black
olives, capers and parsley. When the sauce
simmers, add fish fillets. Spoon sauce over
fish. Cover partially and simmer over low
heat 20 minutes or until the fish is cooked.

The landscape of the Lombard lake district has a climate
part Mediterranean and part Alpine. It is one of the most
elegant areas of Italy. This special menu might be served
in the beautiful garden of a palatial lakeside villa.

MENU:

Aperitivo (Prosecco)
Prosciutto with Melon
Risotto
Veal Cutlets with Hazelnuts
Marinated Zucchini with Fresh Mint
Radicchio Ribbon Salad
Fruit and Cheese
Chilled Gavi or Orvieto
Espresso

MAKES 4 TO 5 SERVINGS

Grilled Salmon
with Pesto

The scent of fresh basil perfumes the air along the coast of Liguria. Local legends tell of sailors who prepared staples of pesto for long sea voyages. One of those culinarians may have been the Genovese seafarer, Christopher Columbus. To create a stunning dish, place each portion of salmon on a nest of Farfalle in Sun-Dried Tomato Sauce, page 31.

1/3 CUP PESTO, PAGE 21

1 TABLESPOON FRESH LEMON JUICE

2 POUNDS OR 4 SALMON FILLETS (ABOUT 8 OUNCES EACH)

SALT AND FRESHLY GROUND BLACK PEPPER, TO TASTE

2 TABLESPOONS OLIVE OIL

Prepare pesto; stir in lemon juice. Season fillets with salt and pepper. Heat oil in a large skillet over medium-high heat. Sear fillets 2 minutes on each side or until the salmon begins to flake. Do not overcook; fish should remain moist and soft in the center. Remove fillets to heated serving plates. Spread each hot fillet with one generous tablespoon of pesto. Serve immediately.

ITALIAN MEALS

Secondo piatto, or the "second plate," is usually fish, meat or poultry, accompanied by the contorno, a carefully chosen vegetable dish, or perhaps a refreshing salad. Bread and wine are served throughout the meal. Finally, fruit, cheese, espresso and a dolce or sweet are served to complete the meal.

MAKES 4 SERVINGS

Chicken Breasts with Prosciutto and Fontina

Such wonderful flavors! The red pepper strips create a colorful design under the melted cheese. For an additional taste surprise, spread each sautéed chicken breast with one teaspoon of olivada (olive paste) or pesto before the prosciutto and cheese are added. This recipe multiplies easily.

2 WHOLE CHICKEN BREASTS, CUT IN HALF, SKINNED, BONED

1 TABLESPOON BUTTER

1 TABLESPOON OLIVE OIL

SALT AND FRESHLY GROUND BLACK PEPPER, TO TASTE

1 OR 2 TABLESPOONS MINCED FRESH HERBS (BASIL, MARJORAM, THYME, ROSEMARY)

4 THIN SLICES PROSCIUTTO OR HAM

1 LARGE ROASTED RED BELL PEPPER, PAGE 11, CUT IN STRIPS

4 THIN SLICES FONTINA OR PROVOLONE CHEESE

Preheat oven broiler. To flatten chicken breasts, pound each piece between 2 pieces of waxed paper. Heat butter and oil in a large skillet. Sauté chicken breasts 2 minutes on each side, until almost done. Remove chicken breasts to an ovenproof casserole dish; sprinkle with salt, pepper and fresh herbs. Cover each with 1 piece prosciutto and one or two strips of bell pepper. Top each piece with a slice of fontina or provolone. Place pan under the hot broiler 1 minute or until cheese begins to melt. Serve immediately.

MAKES 4 SERVINGS

Grilled Lamb Chops
with Mint Pesto

Garden-fresh mint pesto is delicious served with lamb
chops or rubbed over a leg of lamb before roasting.
For the finest flavor and texture, the lamb chops
should remain slightly pink in the center. Extra pesto
can be thinned with balsamic vinegar for a tasty
sauce. Spoon over portions of cooked lamb.

1 PACKED CUP FRESH MINT

1/4 CUP PINE NUTS

2 GARLIC CLOVES

2 TABLESPOONS FRESH
LEMON JUICE OR WHITE
WINE VINEGAR

1/4 TEASPOON SALT

3 TO 4 TABLESPOONS
EXTRA VIRGIN OLIVE OIL

8 LAMB CHOPS, CUT
1-INCH THICK

SALT AND FRESHLY GROUND
BLACK PEPPER, TO TASTE

In a food processor fitted with the steel blade,
process mint, pine nuts, garlic, lemon juice and salt.
Add olive oil; process until a paste is formed.
Scrape mixture into a small bowl. Prepare charcoal
fire with fragrant hardwoods. Rub the lamb chops
with 3 tablespoons of pesto. Grill 4 to 5 minutes on
each side for medium-rare. Remove from grill; add
salt and pepper. Serve immediately.

MAKES 4 SERVINGS

VERDUE E INSALATA

- vegetables and salads -

DENISE'S STUFFED
ARTICHOKES

ROSEMARY
POTATOES WITH
ONIONS, PEPPERS
AND OLIVES

RADICCHIO
RIBBON SALAD

BRAISED
ESCAROLE

GERRIE'S SAUTÉED
PEPPERS AND
TOMATOES

TUSCAN BEAN
SALAD WITH SAGE

BAKED TOMATOES
WITH BASIL
AND PARMESAN

Denise's Stuffed Artichokes

Denise Michaels serves these delicious stuffed artichokes as a vegetable course. During the holidays, her Sicilian family enjoys an antipasto of small stuffed artichokes. Denise peels and simmers the stems with the large artichokes. When tender, she purées them with garlic, lemon and seasonings for a tasty sauce for chicken or veal. Sometimes she whips them into mashed potatoes with garlic and chicken stock.

3 GARLIC CLOVES, MINCED	1 TEASPOON GARLIC SALT OR POWDER
2 CUPS SEASONED BREAD CRUMBS	1 TEASPOON ONION SALT
1/3 CUP OLIVE OIL	2 TABLESPOONS FRESHLY GRATED PECORINO CHEESE
1 1/2 TEASPOONS SALT, OR TO TASTE	4 CUPS WATER
1 TEASPOON PEPPER	4 LARGE ARTICHOKES

Combine all ingredients, except water and artichokes, in a medium bowl; set aside. Pour water into a 4-quart pot. Cut off artichoke stems. Peel off the first layer of small tough leaves around the bottoms. Cut 1/4-inch off the top of each artichoke. Rinse under cool water, spreading the leaves. Shake off excess water. To stuff, lightly fill each leaf with reserved bread crumb mixture. Place stuffed artichokes into the water. Cover and bring to a boil. After 5 minutes, reduce heat to low; simmer 50 to 55 minutes. Artichokes are done when a leaf can easily be tugged out. Serve warm or cold.

MAKES 4 SERVINGS

Rosemary Potatoes with Onions, Peppers and Olives

To fully appreciate the flavors in this
dish, allow it to cool a few minutes
before serving. Substitute oregano,
thyme or sage for the rosemary.

4 TABLESPOONS OLIVE
OIL, OR AS NEEDED

4 OR 5 LARGE YUKON
GOLD POTATOES, CUT IN
1/4 INCH-THICK SLICES

1 MEDIUM RED ONION, CUT
IN HALF, THINLY SLICED

1 MEDIUM YELLOW
BELL PEPPER, CUT
IN 1-INCH PIECES

1 LARGE GARLIC
CLOVE, MINCED

1 TO 2 TABLESPOONS
FRESH ROSEMARY LEAVES

4 TABLESPOONS FRESHLY
GRATED PARMESAN CHEESE

1/3 CUP KALAMATA
OLIVES, PITTED

SALT AND FRESHLY GROUND
BLACK PEPPER, TO TASTE

Preheat oven to 350°. Spread 2 tablespoons oil in
the bottom of a large ovenproof casserole pan.
Arrange 1/2 of the potato slices in the pan. Top
with 1/2 of the remaining ingredients in the order
they are listed. Drizzle with 1 tablespoon oil. Add
the remaining half of the ingredients; drizzle with
remaining oil. Cover and bake 40 minutes. Remove
lid. Cook 15 minutes or until the top is crusty.

MAKES 6 SERVINGS

Radicchio Ribbon Salad

Red verona chicory, the type of radicchio found in most American markets, resembles heads of baby cabbage. Radicchio ribbons add a colorful, festive accent to this salad. Split heads of radicchio are delicious brushed with olive oil and grilled for a salad or vegetable course. Another popular Italian salad bowl lettuce is lollo rossa. Dubbed "lollo" for Lollobrigida, this lettuce has attractive curvaceous leaves!

6 CUPS MIXED TORN SALAD GREENS (ROMAINE, SPINACH, ARUGULA, FENNEL LEAVES)

1 SMALL HEAD RADICCHIO, RINSED, PATTED DRY, CUT IN 1/4-INCH STRIPS

1/2 SMALL RED ONION, QUARTERED, CUT IN PAPER-THIN SLICES

1/4 CUP TOASTED PINE NUTS

2 OUNCES SHREDDED RICOTTA SALATA, CRUMBLED FETA OR GORGONZOLA CHEESE

VINAIGRETTE:

1/3 CUP EXTRA VIRGIN OLIVE OIL

2 TABLESPOONS BALSAMIC VINEGAR

1 CLOVE GARLIC, MINCED

SALT, TO TASTE

Toss salad ingredients in a large bowl. In a small bowl, whisk oil, vinegar, garlic and salt. Sprinkle over greens; toss well. Serve immediately.

MAKES 6 SERVINGS

Braised Escarole

Some vegetable dishes are so satisfying, they become a light meal in themselves. Gerrie Cascione shared this simple effective method for preparing escarole, chicory or even broccoli. Rinse the greens well to remove every trace of sandy soil that might be trapped between the leaves.

3 BUNCHES FRESH ESCAROLE OR CHICORY, RINSED, TRIMMED, CUT IN HALF

1 MEDIUM ONION, THINLY SLICED

1 LARGE FRESH TOMATO, DICED, OR 1/4 CAN CRUSHED TOMATOES

1/2 TEASPOON MINCED GARLIC

1 TABLESPOON MINCED FRESH PARSLEY

2 TABLESPOONS OLIVE OIL

2 BEEF BOUILLON CUBES, CRUSHED

10 TABLESPOONS FRESHLY GRATED PARMESAN CHEESE

Cook escarole in boiling salted water, about 10 minutes. Drain and cool slightly; press out excess water. Set aside. Place the onion, tomato, garlic, parsley, oil, bouillon cubes and 2 tablespoons Parmesan cheese in a large saucepan. Add 1 cup water. Place escarole halves on top of the ingredients; cover with remaining cheese. Partially cover pan. Simmer over medium-low heat for 1/2 hour. Do not turn escarole; occasionally push the greens down into the broth with a large spoon.

MAKES 6 SERVINGS

Gerrie's Sautéed Peppers and Tomatoes

Here is another quick, delicious dish from Gerrie Cascione, an expert Italian cook. Gerrie learned to prepare treasured family recipes by "watching her Italian mother-in-law cook, who learned by watching her mother, and so on...." The family is from Bari, off the coast of the Adriatic Sea. For a quick meal, serve with crusty Italian bread, black olives and a wedge of cheese.

10 LARGE RED
BELL PEPPERS

1/3 CUP OLIVE OIL

2 POUNDS FRESH
VINE-RIPE TOMATOES,
PEELED AND FINELY
CHOPPED, OR 1
(28-OUNCE) CAN
CRUSHED TOMATOES

SALT, TO TASTE

Trim tops off peppers. Cut open and discard seeds and veins. Cut each pepper into 6 strips. Heat oil in a large pan or wok over medium heat. Add peppers and stir 1 minute. Cover pan. Allow peppers to steam 3 or 4 minutes. Peppers should soften yet retain their shape. Add tomatoes and cook 10 minutes. Salt to taste.

MAKES 6 SERVINGS

Tuscan Bean Salad
with Sage

Cannellini (white kidney) beans provide the mild background flavor for the crunchy, tangy, zesty ingredients in this dish. Serve this rustic salad with grilled meats or sausages. For a satisfying single-course meal, mix in a jar of imported drained tuna. Serve in a soup plate with crusty Italian bread. Do not add salt until beans are half cooked, or they will become tough.

1 1/4 CUPS DRIED CANNELLINI BEANS, OR 1/2 POUND GREAT NORTHERN BEANS, SOAKED OVERNIGHT, OR 2 (19-OUNCE) CANS CANNELLINI BEANS, DRAINED, RINSED

1 LARGE RED ONION, SLICED

SALT AND FRESHLY GROUND BLACK PEPPER, TO TASTE

3 OR 4 FRESH SAGE LEAVES, MINCED

1 LARGE GARLIC CLOVE, MINCED

1 STALK CELERY, DICED

1 SMALL CUCUMBER, PEELED, SEEDED, DICED

5 CHERRY TOMATOES, QUARTERED

1/4 CUP BRINE-CURED BLACK OLIVES, PITTED, COARSELY CHOPPED

1/4 CUP EXTRA VIRGIN OLIVE OIL

3 TABLESPOONS LEMON JUICE OR RED WINE VINEGAR

Drain soaked beans. Place beans and onion in a medium pot; cover with 2 quarts of water. Simmer 30 minutes. Add salt and pepper. Cook 30 minutes more or until tender but not mushy. Drain. Place in a large bowl. When cool, stir in the remaining ingredients. Serve at room temperature.

MAKES 6 SERVINGS

Baked Tomatoes with Basil and Parmesan

Late-summer tomatoes are intensely sweet and taste great. Serve the baked tomatoes as a side dish or chop into coarse pieces and toss with $1/2$ pound of cooked thin spaghetti. Season with salt, pepper and extra grated cheese. For a Neapolitan touch, include 2 or 3 chopped anchovies.

3 LARGE VINE-RIPE TOMATOES (ABOUT 1 $1/2$ POUNDS), CUT IN HALF

$3/4$ CUP DRY GRATED BREAD CRUMBS (12 TABLESPOONS)

2 GARLIC CLOVES, FINELY MINCED

$1/4$ CUP MINCED FRESH HERBS (BASIL, PARSLEY, MARJORAM)

$3/4$ CUP SHREDDED PARMESAN OR ASIAGO CHEESE (12 TABLESPOONS)

6 TABLESPOONS OLIVE OIL

SALT AND FRESHLY GROUND BLACK PEPPER, TO TASTE

Preheat oven to 350°. Put tomatoes in an oiled baking dish, cut sides up. Combine remaining ingredients and sprinkle each tomato with an equal portion. Bake 30 minutes or until crusty. Tomatoes will be soft yet hold a shape.

MAKES 6 SERVINGS

PIZZA E PAN

- pizza and hearth breads -

PIZZA BY THE METER	POTATO FOCACCIA
PIZZA DOUGH	PANINI WITH PROSCIUTTO AND FONTINA
CHUNKY TOMATO SAUCE	

Pizza by the Meter

Born in Naples, pizza is a popular street snack baked in wood-burning ovens. Carbonized loaves of bread, a forebear of pizza, have been dug from the ruins of Pompeii, buried under the ash of Vesuvius. My sister Dee often frequented Italian pizzerie where elongated pizzas were sold by the meter! Pizza with tomato, mozzarella and basil are called Pizza Margherita, after Italy's Queen Margherita. Pizza alla Napoletana includes anchovies.

1 RECIPE CHUNKY TOMATO SAUCE, PAGE 52

1 RECIPE PIZZA DOUGH, PAGE 51

2 TO 3 TABLESPOONS EXTRA VIRGIN OLIVE OIL (HERB FLAVORED, IF AVAILABLE)

3 GARLIC CLOVES, FINELY MINCED

2 TO 3 CUPS MOZZARELLA CHEESE, SHREDDED ($1/2$ TO $3/4$ POUND)

Prepare tomato sauce; set aside. Prepare dough; shape it into a 12-inch by 17-inch baking pan. Brush with oil; let rise 15 minutes. Preheat oven to 450°. Spread dough with tomato sauce. Scatter garlic and cheese on top. Place pan on the lower oven rack or tiles and bake 12 to 15 minutes or until the crust is crisp and brown. Cut into squares; eat the pizza hot.

PIZZA TOPPINGS: Include one or more of these toppings to create your own signature pizza.

$3/4$ cup oil-packed sun-dried tomatoes, cut in strips

$1/2$ cup crumbled gorgonzola cheese

$1/2$ cup Parmesan cheese

$1/4$ pound prosciutto or ham, cut in thin strips

$1/2$ cup imported black or green olives, pitted, chopped

6 ounces cooked artichoke hearts, chopped

Sautéed wild mushrooms, page 17

2 Tablespoons chopped fresh herbs (basil, marjoram, oregano, thyme)

1 medium eggplant, thinly sliced, salted, grilled

1 small red onion, cut in half, thinly sliced

$3/4$ pound cooked crumbled Italian sausage, drained

1 large roasted red bell pepper, page 11, cut in thin strips

MAKES 1 LARGE RECTANGULAR PIZZA
OR 2 SMALL ROUND PIZZAS.

Pizza Dough

Pizza bread is a descendant of the early Roman flat breads.
Two hints for good crust: (1) Line the oven with unglazed
tiles to resemble the interior of a wood-burning oven.
(2) Preheat the oven and tiles to 450° for 15 minutes.

1 ENVELOPE ACTIVE DRY YEAST (2 1/4 TEASPOONS)	3 TABLESPOONS OLIVE OIL (BASIL OR ROSEMARY FLAVORED, IF AVAILABLE)
1/4 TEASPOON SUGAR	3 1/2 TO 4 CUPS BREAD FLOUR
1 1/4 CUPS WARM WATER (110°)	SEMOLINA OR FINE CORNMEAL, AS NEEDED
1 1/2 TEASPOONS SALT	PIZZA TOPPINGS, PAGE 50

Dissolve yeast and sugar in water in a large mixing bowl. Proof 5
minutes or until foamy. Stir in salt, oil, and 2 cups flour. Mix well.
Add 1 1/2 cups flour; stir until a slightly sticky ball of dough
forms. Knead 5 minutes on a lightly floured surface until smooth
and elastic. Coat with oil; place in a large bowl. Cover; let rise
until doubled, about 2 hours. Punch down. If making 2 pies,
divide in half. Let dough rest 10 minutes. Flatten dough on pan;
gently pull and stretch to fit pan. If dough is resistant, wait 5
minutes; begin again. Work dough to edges. Press to form a small
rim. Or, shape dough on a lightly floured surface. Place on a pizza
peel dusted with semolina. Brush with oil. Preheat oven to 450°.
Let dough rest 15 minutes. Add toppings. Place pan on bottom
oven rack or heated tiles. If pizza is on a peel, slide onto tiles.
Bake 10 minutes or until crust is crisp and lightly browned.

TIP: Pizza al Quattro Formaggi is a splendid pizza drizzled with
olive oil and topped with a blend of four aristocratic Italian
cheeses: Parmigiano, fontina, mozzarella and gorgonzola.

MAKES DOUGH FOR 2 ROUND PIZZAS, 1 12-INCH BY
17-INCH OBLONG PIZZA OR 8 5-INCH ROUND PIZZAS.

Chunky Tomato Sauce

Tomatoes made their way from South America to Italy in the 16th century; they flourished in southern Italy's hot nurturing sun. Fresh juicy tomato chunks or slices taste superb on pizza. This recipe produces a rich concentrated sauce made from canned tomatoes, perfect when vine-ripened tomatoes are hard to come by. For the best sauce use top-quality imported or domestic canned Roma tomatoes; try the imported San Marzano brand.

1/4 CUP OLIVE OIL	1 TABLESPOON MINCED FRESH BASIL OR OREGANO LEAVES
4 GARLIC CLOVES, THINLY SLICED	1/2 TEASPOON SALT, OR TO TASTE
1 (28-OUNCE) CAN QUALITY PLUM TOMATOES, DRAINED, COARSELY CHOPPED	TWO TO THREE DASHES OF FRESHLY GROUND PEPPER

Heat oil in a medium saucepan over medium-low heat. Add garlic, stir and cook 30 seconds. Do not brown. Add tomatoes; simmer 20 minutes or until liquid is reduced. Stir in basil, salt and pepper; cook 1 minute more. Cool before using.

TIPS: Refrigerate the drained juice from canned tomatoes to enrich dishes such as soups, stews or meatloaf. Freeze in 1 cup amounts for longer storage.

In central and southern Italian restaurants, bread is served with small bowls of olive oil for dipping. Tuscan diners dip their unsalted bread, then sprinkle it with salt. In some regions, the oil is seasoned with herbs or chilies.

MAKES 2 CUPS

Potato Focaccia

Focaccia is a rustic hearth bread from the Ligurian
region of Genoa. It is baked throughout Italy, with
different names and in a variety of shapes. Focacce can
be soft, crispy, thick or thin. The dough contains more
oil than pizza dough. You can divide the dough and
bake in thin loaves on 2 jelly roll pans. Top with grated
cheese, herbs, sliced onions, prosciutto or salami.

1 ENVELOPE DRY YEAST (2 $1/4$ TEASPOONS)	2 TEASPOONS SALT
$1/2$ TEASPOON SUGAR	$1/2$ CUP PLAIN OR HERB-FLAVORED OLIVE OIL PLUS EXTRA FOR TOPPING
1 CUP WATER, HEATED TO 110° (PLUS 1 CUP POTATO WATER)	
1 CUP FRESH UNSEASONED MASHED POTATO	6 $1/2$ TO 7 CUPS UNBLEACHED ALL-PURPOSE FLOUR, AS NEEDED

Dissolve yeast and sugar in 1 cup warm water in a large mixing
bowl. Proof 5 minutes or until foamy. Add potato water, potato,
salt and olive oil. With a heavy mixer, slowly beat in flour. Soft
dough will form a sticky ball. Knead 3 minutes until smooth and
elastic. Scrape onto a lightly floured surface. Knead 30 seconds. Oil
dough lightly and place in a large bowl. Cover. Let rise until doubled, about 2 hours. Oil a 17-inch by 11-inch baking pan. Flatten
dough on pan; gently pull and stretch to fit pan. Work dough to
the edges. Cover. Let rise 30 minutes. With fingers, press indenta-
tions into dough. Brush with oil. Cover lightly with a tea towel and
let rise 1 hour. Preheat oven to 375°. Bake 20 minutes or until
golden brown. Brush with oil; cool completely on a rack, if possi-
ble. Cut in strips or squares. Wrap leftovers; rewarm if desired.

MAKES 10 TO 12 SERVINGS

Panini with Prosciutto and Fontina

Panini, or sandwiches, are an important part of Italy's snacking tradition. This panino features focaccia, a type of flat bread. The sandwiches are great for lunch, picnics or cut in small portions for parties. Other ingredients might include Genoa salami, marinated artichoke hearts, capers or chopped black olives. The sandwiches are delicious at room temperature, heated in the oven or grilled.

4 4-INCH SQUARES OF POTATO FOCACCIA, PAGE 53

2 TO 3 TEASPOONS PESTO, PAGE 21, TO TASTE

1/3 CUP GOOD-QUALITY MAYONNAISE

8 THIN SLICES PROSCIUTTO OR BAKED HAM

4 THIN SLICES FONTINA, PROVOLONE OR SWISS CHEESE

2 OR 3 RIPE ROMA TOMATOES OR 1 RIPE ROUND TOMATO, THINLY SLICED

12 ARUGULA LEAVES OR BIBB LEAVES OR WATERCRESS, RINSED, PATTED DRY

With a serrated knife, slice bread in half horizontally. Stir pesto into mayonnaise; spread inside each bread square. Stuff each piece with two slices of prosciutto, a slice of cheese, tomato slices and 3 arugula leaves. Serve at once or wrap loosely in plastic wrap for 1 or 2 hours. Wrap securely in plastic wrap to transport to a picnic.

In the Tuscan countryside, you might discover a similar picnic fare spread on a blanket under lovely azure blue skies. Close your eyes and feel the warm breezes rustling through the olive trees, smell the perfume of fragrant citrus trees and hear the spirited, sing-song Italian voices toasting the day with glasses of robust red wine.

AL FRESCO PICNIC:

Panini with Prosciutto and Fontina

Tuscan Bean Salad with Sage

Hazelnut-Spice Biscotti

A basket of peaches and strawberries

Chianti Classico

Acqua minerale

MAKES 4 SERVINGS

I DOLCI

- sweets and fruits -

THE GRAND FINALE	AMARETTO BREAD PUDDING
HAZELNUT-SPICE BISCOTTI	ESPRESSO CREAM CAKE
A CUP OF ESPRESSO	RASPBERRY BRUSCHETTA

The Grand Finale

A special Italian meal ends on just the right note. For Tres Marie D'Agostino's Sicilian family, dessert is a symphony of courses that are easy to duplicate. A refreshing bowl of mixed fresh fruit immediately follows the meal. Bite-size pieces of melon, red or white grapes, berries, oranges, apples or peaches are macerated in a little liqueur such as kirsch or grappa—Italian brandy.

On the sideboard is espresso with after-dinner liqueurs such as rum, cognac, anisette or Sambuca, made from elder. (Elder flowers were commonly used in Italian dishes during the Middle Ages.) A tantalizing array of biscotti (cookies), small pastries and nuts are arranged on trays. You might offer ready-made sweets such as amaretti (almond cookies), torrone (nougat), confetti (sugar-coated almonds) or chocolates such as baci, chocolate hazelnut "kisses."

Fruit and cheese make a beautiful pairing! For an informal meal offer an array of seasonal fresh fruits: plums, berries, grapes, dates, figs or pears. Add a wedge of dolce latte (sweet gorgonzola) or a pot of sweetened mascarpone and brandied cherries. Serve with walnuts, crackers or brioche. A glass of sweet marsala or Asti Spumanti would be equally welcomed.

Hazelnut-Spice Biscotti

This type of cookie is "twice baked" until crisp and dry. It is designed to be dipped into sweet white wine or steaming hot cappuccino; perfect for breakfast or merenda (snack time). The cookies can be made with hazelnuts or a combination of hazelnuts and walnuts, in which case I use a blend of light olive oil and walnut oil. The cookies can be drizzled with melted chocolate.

2 LARGE EGGS (PLUS 1 EGG, SEPARATED)

1/3 CUP LIGHT OLIVE OIL OR SAFFLOWER OIL

1 1/2 CUPS SUGAR

GRATED RIND OF 1 ORANGE

1 TEASPOON GROUND CINNAMON

1/2 TEASPOON EACH GROUND CLOVES, MACE AND GINGER

1 TABLESPOON COFFEE LIQUEUR OR DARK RUM

2 TEASPOONS BAKING POWDER

2 1/2 CUPS HAZELNUTS, LIGHTLY TOASTED

3 CUPS ALL-PURPOSE FLOUR, LIGHTLY SPOONED INTO MEASURING CUP

Preheat oven to 350°. In a large bowl, beat 2 eggs plus 1 yolk with the oil and sugar. Stir in orange rind, spices, liqueur, baking powder and nuts. Add flour; stir until dough is formed. Divide in half and place on a 17-inch by 11-inch oiled baking sheet. Shape dough into 2 thin loaves, 2-inches wide, 15-inches long. Loaves should be at least 2 inches apart. Brush lightly with egg white. Bake 25 minutes. Carefully cut warm loaves into 1-inch slices; lift gently and spread over 2 baking sheets. Reduce heat to 275°. Bake 12 to 15 minutes or until crisp and dry. Cool; store in a tin.

A CUP OF ESPRESSO: Espresso is a richly concentrated, dark coffee, served in small portions. In Italy, it is usually referred to it as caffé (coffee). A cup of espresso is a great pick-me-up during the day and the perfect ending for a fine meal. Espresso ristretto, made with half the amount of water as espresso, is even more concentrated. Cappuccino is made with equal parts espresso and milk; the top dense with milk foam. A cup of espresso embellished with a tablespoon of a liqueur is called caffé corretto, or "corrected" coffee.

MAKES ABOUT 30 COOKIES

Amaretto Bread Pudding

In the 16th century, an Italian innkeeper's wife modeled for Bernardino Luini, Leonardo's favorite student. He captured her beauty in a portrait of the Madonna. She thanked him with a gift of homemade almond liqueur made from apricot kernels. The liqueur, Amaretto de Soronna, is featured in this delicious bread pudding, a specialty of Villa Tronco. This fine Italian restaurant in Columbia, South Carolina, was founded by Sadie Tronco during World War II when she served spaghetti to homesick soldiers of Italian descent stationed at Fort Jackson.

1 LOAF ITALIAN OR FRENCH BREAD, BROKEN INTO SMALL PIECES	1 1/2 CUPS SUGAR
1 QUART HALF AND HALF	2 TABLESPOONS PURE ALMOND EXTRACT
2 TABLESPOONS UNSALTED BUTTER, ROOM TEMPERATURE	3/4 CUP GOLDEN RAISINS
3 LARGE EGGS	3/4 CUP SLICED ALMONDS
	AMARETTO SAUCE, BELOW

Place bread in a medium bowl; add half and half. Cover; let stand 1 hour. Preheat oven to 325°. Grease a 9-inch by 13-inch baking pan with the butter. In a small bowl, beat eggs, sugar and almond extract. Stir into bread mixture. Gently fold in raisins and almonds. Spread bread mixture evenly into baking dish. Set on the middle oven rack and bake 50 minutes until golden. Remove and cool. Prepare Amaretto Sauce. Preheat broiler. Cut pudding into 8 to 10 squares; place on a decorative ovenproof serving dish. Spoon sauce over pudding. Place under broiler until sauce bubbles. Serve immediately.

AMARETTO SAUCE: 1 stick unsalted butter (8 Tablespoons), at room temperature 1 cup confectioners' sugar 1 egg, well beaten 1/4 cup Amaretto liqueur	Combine butter and sugar in the top part of a double boiler. Stir constantly until butter melts and sugar dissolves. Remove from heat. Rapidly whisk egg into hot sugar mixture. Continue whisking until the sauce comes to room temperature. Stir in Amaretto liqueur.

MAKES 8 TO 10 SERVINGS.

Espresso Cream Cake

Sweetness is the Italian flavor of passion and delight. This luscious cake is especially creamy and light; goat cheese adds a special richness. Some brands of ricotta are very wet. If your brand does not hold its shape when unmolded, drain it to firm it up. The cream filling can be served as pudding with berries or as a luxurious dip for almond toast cookies

1 CUP RICOTTA CHEESE

4 OUNCES SEMISWEET OR WHITE CHOCOLATE, FINELY CHOPPED (TOBLER OR LINDT)

8 OUNCES CREAM CHEESE, ROOM TEMPERATURE

2 OUNCES FRESH, MILD GOAT CHEESE, ROOM TEMPERATURE

1 CUP CONFECTIONERS' SUGAR

1 3/4 CUPS HEAVY CREAM, WHIPPED

2 3-OUNCE PACKAGES LADYFINGERS

1/4 CUP ESPRESSO OR STRONGLY BREWED HAZELNUT COFFEE

1/4 CUP COFFEE LIQUEUR

4 TABLESPOONS CHOPPED TOASTED HAZELNUTS OR SLICED TOASTED ALMONDS

DASH OF CINNAMON

12 CHOCOLATE-COVERED ESPRESSO BEANS

If necessary, spoon ricotta into a colander lined with cheesecloth or a large coffee filter; drain two hours. Sift chocolate chunks to remove chocolate powder; reserve both. With a mixer, beat ricotta, cream cheese, goat cheese and sugar until smooth. By hand, fold in 2 cups whipped cream and chopped chocolate. Brush the flat sides of the ladyfingers with a blend of espresso and coffee liqueur.
Line the sides and bottom of an 8-inch springform pan with ladyfingers, soaked sides inward. Pour in 1/2 the cheese mixture; sprinkle with 1/2 the nuts. Add a layer of soaked ladyfingers. Pour in second half of the cheese mixture; top with remaining whipped cream. Sprinkle with chocolate powder and cinnamon. Chill overnight. Run a knife between pan and cake and gently remove ring. Cut in 12 slices; top each with an espresso bean.

MAKES 12 SERVINGS

Raspberry Bruschetta

This delectable dessert toast should be made with chewy country loaves or crusty baguettes; it will make a difference in the final taste. Mascarpone is a luscious creamy triple-cream cheese; delicious topped with raspberries, strawberries, peaches, brandied cherries, marmalade or grated chocolate. For a delicious low-calorie version, substitute ricotta cheese. Serve sweet bruschetta for breakfast, for dessert or as a snack.

1/2-INCH THICK SLICES OF CRUSTY BREAD, LIGHTLY TOASTED	FRESH RASPBERRIES, BRANDIED CHERRIES, DRAINED, OR OTHER SLICED FRESH FRUITS
MASCARPONE	HONEY

Cool toasted bread a few minutes; spread liberally with mascarpone. Arrange raspberries on top; drizzle lightly with honey. Serve immediately.

TOPPINGS FOR BRUSCHETTA AND MASCARPONE:
Sliced bananas, pine nuts and honey
Sliced fresh peaches, sliced toasted almonds and honey
Sliced fresh dates or figs and chopped toasted walnuts
Orange marmalade and chopped toasted hazelnuts
Poached apple slices, a sprinkle of cinnamon
and a drizzle of maple syrup
Mascarpone blended with orange rind, chopped
chocolate and sliced almonds

NOTE: Piedmont is Italy's region of chocolate production and the home of "gianduia" paste, a delicious blend of chocolate and hazelnuts. You can purchase a yummy chocolate hazelnut spread in the gourmet section of fine markets. It is delicious spread on bread, toast cookies (Stella D'Oro) or rusks.

The Italian Pantry

Several Italian ingredients are indispensable for creating the authentic Italian flavor. If you cannot find one, choose a similar product of fine quality.

– BALSAMIC VINEGAR –

Considered a condiment, balsamic vinegar has a delicate sweet-sour taste. The color is reminiscent of fine old Madeira. It is aged in barrels of descending sizes, with layers of flavor, similar to good wine. Great balsamic is sipped as an aperitif! The best comes from Modena and Reggio Emilia in northern Italy. Handcrafted balsamic can cost $50 an ounce; good vinegar is available for less. A chef's trick to enhance less expensive balsamic is to stir one teaspoon melted dark brown sugar into each cup. A few drops of balsamic add fabulous flavor; some chefs dispense it with an atomizer. Use on grilled fish, vegetables, meats and salads. A few drops on underripe strawberries make them taste freshly picked!

– CAPERS –

Tiny unopened flower buds of the caper bush. Sun-dried and packed in vinegar brine; rinse before use. The smallest are the most intensely flavored. Chop large capers to release their flavor.

– GARLIC –

Indispensable seasoning! For a subtle taste, sauté whole smashed cloves in oil, then discard the cloves. The flavor of minced garlic mellows with long simmering. For more intensity, ing the last 15 minutes of cooking. Mince garlic by hand to release any bitter juices.

– HERBS –

Flat-leaf Italian parsley and basil are popular cooking herbs; curly leaf parsley is a good substitute. In northern Italy, mild marjoram is favored; a stronger cousin, oregano, is popular in the south. Dried oregano has a sweet pungent flavor. Other popular herbs are sage, rosemary, bay leaves and tarragon. Trim fresh herb stems; refrigerate in water 1 week. Preserve in oil, layer in salt in sealed jars or puree into paste with olive oil. If using dried herbs, crushed whole dried leaves add more flavor.

– OLIVES –

Olives can add a range of lively flavors to dishes: tart green Sicilian olives, large mild Greek Kalamata olives, sharper gaeta olives and small refined French Niçoise olives. To remove olive pits, use a large knife to press firmly on each olive to crush and open it.

– OLIVE OIL –

Except in the butter-loving north, olive oil is Italy's primary cooking fat. Extra virgin oil is made from stone-ground olives, cold-pressed without heat or chemicals. Extra virgin oil has a green-gold hue and a fruity, robust flavor. There are different qualities; taste to determine your preference. Use as a condiment for salad, pasta, fish and vegetable dishes. "Pure" olive oil is a milder, all-purpose blend, excellent for frying and other cooking chores. New extra light olive oils are light in flavor, not calories; good for baking. Herb, chili and citrus rind-flavored oils add a touch of panache. Quality oil comes from Tuscany and Umbria; Liguria, on the Italian Riviera, produces fine pale oil, similar to French oil. Heavier, fruity oils come from Calabria. Buy in small amounts; store in a dark, cool place. If your oil is too strong, dilute with a small amount of flavorless canola oil.

- PANCETTA -

Pancetta coppata is cured rolled pork butt, sliced like salami. Pancetta affumicata is the only smoked bacon. Substitute any quality bacon. Too much smoky flavor can be removed through blanching 1 or 2 minutes.

- PASTA -

Fresh and dried pasta have different uses; one is not better than the other. Northerners favor fresh pasta; southerners love dried. Thick fresh pasta sheets are often used for tortellini, lasagna, ravioli and cannelloni. The best imported and domestic pastas are made with 100% hard durum wheat semolina flour. Cooked pasta made with semolina flour almost doubles in volume and does not become mushy if overcooked a minute or two. Its slight roughness coats better with sauce. Long pasta shapes go well with creamy sauces with minced ingredients. Shorter, bulky shapes compliment chunky sauces. Tiny pasta shapes are great for soups. One pound dried pasta serves 4 as a main course and 6 as a first course.

- PROSCIUTTO -

Few tastes are as pleasurable as prosciutto crudo—not smoked, salted, air-dried ham. Prosciutto is pressed to create its silky-fine texture. Safe to eat uncooked. Serve in thin slices but not paper-thin. Refrigerate in plastic wrap; best served within a few hours. Italians eat prosciutto slices with crusty bread and butter, wrapped around melon slices and with figs, dates and pears. Add to sauces, pasta dishes and stuffing. Fine hams from Parma, San Daniele and Veneto may cost $25 a pound; a little goes a long way.

- TOMATOES -

Sweetly ripened tomatoes are one of the pleasures of the Italian kitchen. Fresh plum (Roma) tomatoes are excellent for making sauces and for drying because they have a lower proportion of juice to pulp. Freeze garden-fresh plum tomatoes whole; to use, soak in warm water and then pull off the peels. Wedges of vine-ripened, round tomatoes can be frozen on baking sheets; pop into sturdy bags for freezing up to 6 months. Imported and domestic canned plum tomatoes are a good substitute. Cover leftover tomato paste with olive oil in a jar and refrigerate.

- WINE -

Any wine you would be happy to drink is good for cooking. Dry Sicilian marsala is a favorite for savory Italian dishes. The domestic wine is sweeter; you may wish to substitute dry sherry. Sweet marsala is a dessert wine; good for sweets such as zabaione, an egg and wine pudding.

—Clifton Fadiman

Italian Cheese

- ASIAGO -

Semi-fat cow's milk cheese made in Veneto since the Middle Ages. Excellent for cooking and grating.

- FONTINA -

From the Val d'Aosta, this semi-soft cow's milk cheese has a soft mellow, nutty flavor. It melts beautifully and is used for making fondue, a famous sauce of the Piedmonte area.

- GORGONZOLA -

A creamy, delicious cow's milk cheese with bluish-green veins; named after its place of origin, near Milan. Delicious on pizza, polenta, salads or simmered in cream for pasta. Use Maytag or Danish blue as a substitute.

- GRANA PADANO -

A fine-grained younger cousin of Parmigiano Reggiano, aged from 12 to 24 months. Young grana is a table cheese; aged grana is used primarily for grating. The name is always stamped on the rind.

- MASCARPONE -

Ultra-creamy, triple-cream cheese made from cow's milk. Use in desserts, as a fruit topping or as a spread. Approximate the texture, if not the exquisite taste, by blending cream cheese and cream fraiche.

- MOZZARELLA -

A fresh cheese made from water buffalo milk, popular in southern Italy. Packed in whey, it must be eaten within a day or two. In Caprese salad, it is served with sliced tomatoes, fresh basil and olive oil. Fresh cow's milk mozzarella, in plastic tubs, is often accessible at fine markets; use within 1 week. Packaged, quality mozzarella can be substituted. Low-fat and very digestible, mozzarella is good plain or used in cooking.

- PARMIGIANO-REGGIANO -

The rich nutty flavor of Italy's premier cheese can make an ordinary dish sing! When heated, the taste intensifies, adding flavor depth. From the grana family, Parmigiano is produced in the Parma/Reggio Emilia areas of northern Italy under strict production codes. The name is stamped repeatedly over the rind of every cheese as a guarantee of authenticity. Pass a wedge at the table with a small grater or pre-grate in the kitchen as needed; serve in a small bowl. The shaved curls are delicious in salad and antipasti. Store cheese tightly wrapped in the refrigerator.

- PECORINO -

Popular in central and southern Italy, pecorino is made from sheep's milk and is Italy's oldest known cheese. Aged pecorino is excellent for grating and adds an appealing country flavor to foods. Each region makes its own version; pecorino romano (Rome) and pecorino sardo (Sardinia) are among the best known. Avoid pre-grated domestic romano. Buy chunks of imported pecorino; grate as needed. Locatelli is an excellent brand.

- PROVOLONE -

Mild cow's milk cheese kneaded, stretched and shaped into round, oval and pear shapes. Good for eating plain or melted.

- RICOTTA -

A by-product of cheese making, ricotta ("recooked") is made from whey separated from milk curds. The whey is cooked until ricotta forms. Ricotta has a mild, delicious taste. In Italy, it is made with sheep's milk. It is well-drained in baskets and holds its shape when unmolded. Domestic ricotta packed in cartons is often wetter; some brands have a slightly grainy texture. Polly-O is a good brand. Some Italian-American chefs enrich domestic ricotta with a small amount of mild, fresh goat cheese. Delicious eaten plain or used in savory stuffing, pies, cheesecakes, puddings or cakes.

- RICOTTA SALATA -

Slightly aged sheep's milk cheese with a special flavor. Good for grating or crumbling on pizza, salad or pasta. Feta is a good substitute.